Captain Planet MF Ital Plant Base Cookbook

By Aion Wilson

Ital Cookbook
Eat Healthy Muhfukka

Published by Earthiopia Works for Captain Planet MF

Cover Design by: Jashua Sa-Ra

ISBN: 9781099344169

Acknowledgement

I would like to take a moment to acknowledge the ancestors and thank them for bestowing upon me the divine knowledge of health and wisdom.

Foreward

I made the cookbook because cooking for me is much more than following recipes. It is more about love, being creative, visualizing your next meal, and being able to put together what you want to eat. Allowing yourself to follow your taste buds and your creativity to conjure up anything you want. Honestly, I felt like I had the cheat codes to ital food and health, so I felt that I needed to give y'all the secrets! Nah...scratch that bullshit...we are family...I HAVE to give you the motherfucking secret, even though you might not want it! You can't put recipe on awesome.

My Testimony

How did I go from 410 lbs to 290 lbs in 8 - 12 months (and STILL dropping) by going plant base?

Well here's the thing: I didn't chase weight loss - I chased Health, and therefore the side effects were my body healed itself. Due to this I've lost over 100 pounds.

What made me want to be healthy?

In the year of 2015 I lost two friends due to a heart attack. Ages 34 and 37 male and female (young right?). Who would think someone so young can die from a heart attack at that age? All I could think about is that it could be me! I weighed a grand total of 410 lbs (muscle and fat). I started looking into documentaries such as Food Matters, Fed-up, Cow conspiracy, Forks over Knifes and more. These documentaries made me mentally and physically ready to DO more for my health, and gradually I started to treat my body like a temple.

The main question and everyone's concern is comfortability. **How did I become so comfortable with eating straight plant base coming from angus burgers, oxtails, bacon egg and cheese's, sea food, and all the fast food restaurants?**

I found something within me that I can never lose, and that's where I come from - Jamaica.
Everyone loves flavor, I know I do. I have a Caribbean background, so I used my culture to my advantage to be comfortable with eating plant based, using Jamaican herbs and seasoning in my meals.

With all of that being said, lately I've been spending a lot of time on my non-profit organization, CaptainPlanestMF inc., to build awareness on a plant based lifestyle that can save you from a heart attack today, and many other vital diseases such as cancer, diabetes, high blood pressure, colon cancer and much more. The list is virtually endless with there being more rare diseases currently being discovered with no cure.

WHAT IS ITAL?

Ital or I-tal is food often celebrated by those in the Rastafari movement. It is mandatory in the Nyabinghi mansion, though not in the Twelve Tribes of Israel or Remi mansions. The word derives from the English word "vital," with the initial syllable replaced by "i." This is done to many words in the Rastafari vocabulary to signify the unity of the speaker with all of nature. Rastafari derive their beliefs and morality from intense personal meditations and prayer, therefore there is no single dogma of Rastafari belief. Due to this emphasis on individual personal meditation in Rastafari, the expression of Ital eating varies widely from Rasta to Rasta, and there are few universal "rules" of Ital living. The primary goal of adhering to an Ital diet is to increase Livity, or the life energy that Rastafari generally believe lives within all human beings, as conferred from the Almighty. A common tenet of Rastafari beliefs is the sharing of a central Livity among living things, and what is put into one's body should enhance Livity rather than reduce it. Though there are different interpretations of Ital regarding specific foods, the general principle is that food should be natural, or pure, and from the earth; Rastafari therefore often avoid food which is chemically modified or contains artificial additives. Some also avoid added salt in foods, especially salt with the artificial addition of iodine, while pure sea or kosher salt is eaten by some. In strict interpretations, foods that have been produced using chemicals such as pesticides and fertilizer are not considered Ital.

Note: I only cook with Grapeseed oil because it is meant for high heat (sautéeing, deep frying, etc.)

GLOSSARY OF INGREDIENTS

I prefer to use fresh herbs, because a lot of the benefits have been stripped away in store bought seasoning due to processing.

When I'm cooking I prefer to use dry herbs instead of store bought seasoning; they're fresher. You actually get to taste the robust flavors in onion, turmeric, and the ginger. It adds more love and flavor to your dish. But I did offer some suggested amounts to people who are used to store-bought seasoning.

Ginger is a great replacement for garlic. It relieves muscle pain and settles the stomach. It can help regulate blood sugar, as well as prevents heart disease. It reduces risk of diabetes and cancer. Ginger also eases menstrual pain.

Cayenne pepper is a hot chili pepper. The pepper contains vitamin C, vitamin B6, vitamin E, potassium, manganese, and flavonoids. It has antifungal properties and promotes longevity.

Red onions contain a higher amount of antioxidant compounds than other onions. They are higher in total flavonoids than white onions, while yellow onions are considered to be in the middle.

Cumin is great in its ability to aid in digestion, improve immunity, and treat skin disorders and insomnia. It also helps treat anemia, boils, cancer, and respiratory disorders such as asthma and bronchitis.

Healing herbs

Seamoss /Irish moss
Seamoss is a source of potassium chloride, a nutrient which helps to dissolve catarrhs (inflammation and phlegm in the mucous membranes), which cause congestion. It also contains compounds which act as natural antimicrobial and antiviral agents, helping to get rid of any infections.
Also contains 92 of the 102 minerals that our bodies need, along with Vitamins A, B, C, D, E and K. It is especially rich in calcium and iodine, as well as containing potassium iodide and potassium bromide, selenium, zinc and natural silica

Elderberry
Elderberry is also known for its flavonoids, which stimulate the immune system and have antioxidant properties that can help prevent free radical damage.

Dandelion
The taste of dandelion resembles a slightly bitter green, like arugula. You can eat them fresh in salads, or you could cook them bitches. the best part about eating dandelions just might be the health benefits:
* Highly nutritious
* Contains potent antioxidants
* Helps fight inflammation
* Aids blood sugar control
* Reduces cholesterol
* Lowers blood pressure
* Promotes a healthy liver
* Aids weight loss.

Bladderwrack

Thyroid problems, including an over-sized thyroid gland (goiter). It is also used for obesity, arthritis, joint pain, "hardening of the arteries" (arteriosclerosis), digestive disorders, heartburn, "blood cleansing," constipation, bronchitis, emphysema, urinary tract disorders, and anxiety. Other uses include boosting the immune system and increasing energy.

Chaga Mushroom

Chaga mushroom helps with immunity, respiratory system, anti-cancer, improves stamina, sex drive, and improves liver detoxification

Maca Root Powder

Maca root powder is high in protein and carbs and rich in a number of nutrients, including vitamin C, copper and iron, and also contains many bioactive plant compounds. It increases sex drive in both men and women. Maca root improves your mental well-being and mood by reducing depression and anxiety, especially in menopausal women. Exercise performance is improved, particularly during endurance activities.

Turmeric

Turmeric (especially its most active compound curcumin) has many scientifically-proven health benefits, such as the potential to prevent heart disease, Alzheimer's and cancer. It's a potent anti-inflammatory and antioxidant, and may also help improve symptoms of depression and arthritis.

BASIC RECIPES

How to make your own alkaline water

Ingredients:
1 large Mason Jar
2-3 Key Limes
Tap Water

Instructions:
First put your water on to boil. Once it comes to a boil, turn off heat, and let it set for one more minute. Then pour it into the mason jar to let the rest of the chemicals steam out. When it cools, cut up the key limes and add it to the Mason jar. Let it sit for an hour or two.
Boom! Alkaline water!

To purify your alkaline water add a shungite crystal in the jar and let it sit for 30-60 minutes before drinking.

How to cook Quinoa/Bulgur

Prep Time: 2 mins
Total Time: 22 mins

Ingredients:
1 part uncooked Quinoa (e.g. 1 cup quinoa—any color will do)
2 parts Water (e.g. 2 cups water)

Instructions
Step 1 - Pour the quinoa into a fine mesh colander and rinse under running water for at least 30 seconds. Drain well. This step removes any bitterness on the outside of the quinoa (caused by naturally occurring saponins).
Step 2 - Combine the rinsed quinoa and water in a saucepan. Bring the mixture to a boil over medium-high heat.
Step 3 - When it begins to boil, decrease the heat a bit to maintain a gentle simmer. Cook until the quinoa has absorbed all of the water, about 10 to 20 minutes (small amounts of quinoa will be ready closer to 10 minutes; larger amounts between 15 to 20). Reduce heat as time goes on to maintain a gentle simmer.
Step 4 - Remove the pot from heat, cover, and let the quinoa steam for 5 minutes. This step gives the quinoa time to pop open into little curlicues, so it's nice and fluffy. Remove the lid and fluff the quinoa with a fork.

You will end up with three times as much cooked quinoa.

(Honestly, for my real Cookers out there, fuck the instructions! Pour the quinoa/bulgar in a pot with water and just cook it like rice!)

Spelt dumplings

Serves 4-5 people
Prep Time: 10 mins
Total Time: 22 mins

Ingredients:
1.5 cups of plain, organic Spelt Flour (I use type 500)
1/2 cup of Warm Water
1/2 tsp Pink Himalayan Salt
A few drops of Grapeseed Oil
1/2 tsp Ginger Powder

Instructions
Step 1 - Sift the flour into a bowl, add ginger powder and salt, then mix.
Step 2 - Add the water and a few drops of oil.
Step 3 - Mix thoroughly by hand, and then knead. If the dough is too sticky, add more flour.
Step 4 - Form a ball of it in a bowl covered with damp cloth and leave in the fridge for about 30 minutes.
Step 5 - Then roll the dough into small balls.
Step 6 - Put molded dumplings in salted water and boil for 5 to 7 minutes, until soft.
Put them on plates and decorate as desired.

Sea Moss Gel

1 bag of Sea Moss
1 tsp Vanilla Extract (if you want to flavor it)

Instructions:
Step 1 - Wash half the bag of sea moss.
Step 2 - Leave overnight to soak submerged in water in an open container.
Step 3 - Wash again.
Step 4 - Put in a pot and cover with water.
Step 5 - Boil until it turns into a gel.
Step 5 - Stir in vanilla extract.
Step 6 - Pour into glass bowl or tupperware and refrigerate.

MEAL RECIPES

Spicy Lentil Stew with Chayotes
Serve with fried green plantains

Serves 2-3 people
Prep time: 5 mins
Total time: 25 mins

Ingredients:
½ tsp Ginger
2 Scallion
½ tsp Crushed Chili Peppers
1 Onions
1 bag of Lentils
2 Green Plantains
1 Chayote

Instructions:
Step 1 - Wash your bag of lentils and put them to boil.
Step 2 - Dice up your scallion, ginger, chayote and your plantains (slice them up and put them on the side).
Step 3 - Drain the water from your lentils and put them on the side so they can stop cooking.
Step 4 - Grab your cast iron pan, preheat with Grapeseed oil.
Step 5 - Add all your herbs to the preheated pan so they can start to simmer. A minute after, add the diced up chayote and let it cook for a while before you add the lentils. Just let it simmer (5-6 min).
Step 6 - In a separate pan start frying your green plantain with Grapeseed oil. (Recipe in Snacks and Munchies section)

Spicy Ghana Yam Stew

Serves 4 people
Prep time: 10 mins
Total time: 25 mins

Ingredients:
½ cup Lentils
2 Scallions
1 Ghana Yam
Brussel Sprouts
½ tsp Cayenne Pepper
½ tsp Ginger
½ tsp Crushed Chili Pepper (season to taste)

Instructions:
Step 1 - Wash and put your lentils to boil for 7 mins.
Step 2 - Cut up the brussels sprouts in four small pieces.
Step 3 - Boil the Ghana yam.
Step 4 - Dice up the scallions, ginger add them to your preheated pan on medium fire with the crushed chili pepper.
Step 5 - Add the cooked lentils and brussel sprouts to the sauté.
Step 6 - As soon as the brussels sprouts & lentils are completely cooked, add yam and mix into stew like better.

Spicy Mango Veggie Stir-Fry

Serves 3-4 people
Prep time: 10 mins
Total time: 25 mins

Ingredients:
1 Mango
Brussels Sprouts
String Beans
½ tsp Ginger
½ tsp Turmeric
½ tsp Sea Salt (season to taste)
Grapeseed Oil

Instructions:
Step 1 - Cut up your mango and brussel sprouts. Along with the string bean, mix them together in a plastic bag so they can marinate together.
Step 2 - Wash and cut up the Ghana yam and set them to boil.
Step 3 - Sauté the marinated vegetables in grapeseed oil. Visually make sure the brussel sprouts are cooked, then add the kale to the final product and let them simmer together.
Step 4 - Plate and enjoy.

Raw Kale Salad

Serves 4 people
Prep time: 2 mins
Total time: 5 mins

Ingredients:
2 bunches of Kale
1 bunch of Dandelion Greens
1 Head Purple Cabbage
1 bunch of Watercress
1 Cucumber
1 Red Onion
1 Tomato
½ Tsp Sesame Seeds
Tamarind Dressing (recipe at back of book)

Instructions:
Step 1 - Chop up the purple cabbage, dandelion, kale and the watercress.
Step 2 - Dice up cucumber, onion, and tomato.
Step 3 - Mix it all together and top it with sesame seeds.
Step 4 - Add dressing to taste.

Brussel Sprout Salad

Serves 3 people
Prep time: 5 mins
Total time: 10 mins

Ingredients:
1 bag of Brussels Sprouts
2 Cucumber
1 bag of Pumpkin Seeds
1 Red and Blue Cabbage
1 bunch Watercress
1 bag Mung Beans
1 bunch Dandelion with a nice Tamarind dressing (you can use any dressing you like)

Instructions:
Step 1 - Dice or chop up your ingredients, add it to a bowl.
Step 2 - Make the Tamarind dressing (recipe the back of the book).

Sweet and Spicy Veggie Stir-Fry
Serve with whole wheat bulgar

Serves 4-5 people
Prep Time: 10 mins
Total Time: 22 minutes

Ingredients:
1 bag of Brussel Sprouts
1 lb bag String Beans
1 lb bag of Green Peas
2 Yellow Zucchini
5 Dates
½ Ginger
½ tsp Cumin
½ tsp Chili Pepper
1 Onion

Instructions:
Step 1 - Wash and cut up the brussels sprouts, zucchini, and string beans.
Step 2 - Dice up your dates along with the ginger and onions.
Step 3 - Sauté the dates, ginger, and onion first with the cumin and the chili pepper to get the flavors going.
Step 4 - Wash and boil the whole wheat bulgur (recipe in Basic Recipes section).
Step 5 - Add the brussel sprouts, string beans, green peas and yellow zucchini to the sauté pot.
Step 6 - Let the vegetables sauté till you get a nice brown consistency.

Collard Stir-Fry
Serve with pan-seared Green plantain wedges

Serve 4-5 people
Prep Time: 10 mins
Total Time: 30 minutes

Ingredients:
2 bunches of Collard Greens
½ lb bag of String Beans
1 can Chickpeas
1 inch of Ginger (minced)
1 Onions
½ tsp Cayenne Pepper (season to taste)

If you are using canned beans: wash off all that preservative and sugar before you add to your stir-fry

Instructions:
Step 1 - Grab the two bunches of collard greens, cut and wash them, and put them to boil.
Step 2 - Wash one can of chickpeas in cold water and put on the side to dry.
Step 3 - Cut and prepare green plantains (details in the Snacks and Munchies section).
Step 4 - Check to see if the collard greens are halfway cooked.
Step 5 - Dice up the ginger, onions, and scallion and add them to your preheated pan on medium.
Step 6 - Add the dried chickpeas to the sauté pan with the cooked collard greens to sauté and simmer together with the string beans.

Veggie Lo Mein

Serve 4-5 people
Prep Time: 10 mins
Total Time: 30 minutes

Ingredients:

3 Sweet peppers
½ tsp Ginger
½ tsp Turmeric
1 bunch Collard Greens
1 box Durum Wheat Spaghetti
Sweet Heat Date Sauce (recipe is in back of the book)

Instructions:

Step 1 - Cut and wash 1 bunch of collard greens then put them to boil. Drain and put them on the side when they are tender.

Step 2 - Put water on to boil. Once it comes to a boil, put durum wheat spaghetti in for 7-8 mins. Once done rinse in cold water and put it on the side.

Step 3 - Dice up the sweet pepper, tumeric and ginger and add those to your preheated pan on medium heat.

Step 4 - Add cooked collard greens to the sauté pan. Let the vegetables and herbs simmer together.

Step 5 - Add the spaghetti to the sauté pan and mix it together. Add additional seasoning if desired.

Veggie Alfredo
(no milk no yeast)

Serves 3-4 people
Prep time: 10 mins
Total time: 25 mins

Ingredients:

1 can Butter Beans
1 small bag Cashews
1 bag String Beans
1 bag Sweet Peppers
1 Onion
1 bunch of Kale
1 bunch of Asparagus
½ Cayenne Pepper
½ tsp Ginger
1 box Small Spelt Shells
and the sauce was ▨▨▨▨▨▨▨▨

Instructions:
Step 1 - Soak cashews for two hours.
Step 2 - Wash your butter beans, put them on the side to dry.
Step 3 - Cut up the herbs and vegetables.
Step 4 - Put on a pot of water to boil. Once it comes to a boil, add spelt shells for 7-8 mins. Drain them when finished boiling and put them on the side to cool.
Step 5 - Add the soaked cashews to the butter beans with ginger, paprika, and grapeseed oil in a blender. Blend until you get a nice creamy sauce.
Step 6 - Sauté herbs and vegetables, then add the spelt shells and the cashew cream sauce. Add salt if desired.

Plant Base Quinoa Bowl

Serves 3-4 people
Prep time: 10 mins
Total time: 25 mins

Ingredients:
½ lb Brussel Sprouts
½ lb String Beans
½ cup Craisins
1 Ginger
1 Onions
1 Scallion
A dash of Sea Salt (not iodized)
Sweet Heat Sauce

Instructions:
Step 1 - Wash and put quinoa to boil (recipe in Basic Recipes section).

Step 2 - Dice up your brussel sprouts into quarters (four pieces).

Step 3 - Grab your nonstick pan and coat the bottom with grapeseed oil, then put it on medium heat.

Step 4 - Add diced up ginger, onions, and scallions to the preheated pan with the craisins to simmer.

Step 5 - Add the brussel sprouts and the string beans; continue to sauté and simmer.

Step 6 - Put the cooked quinoa in a bowl with your stir fry and mix them together.

Step 7 - Add the Sweet Heat Date sauce (recipe in Sauces section).

Black Eyed Peas Stir-Fry

Serves 3 people
Prep time: 5 mins
Total time: 20 mins

Ingredients:
½ lb String Bean
1 bunch of Kale
1 can Black Eyed Peas
1 Onion
1 Ginger
Craisins
½ Cayenne Pepper
3 Plantains (mashed "potatoes")
Serve with Sweet Heat Date sauce

Instructions:
Step 1 - Grab the plantains, slice off the ends put them to boil.

Step 2 - Open and wash the black eyed peas. Put them on the side to dry.

Step 3 - Dice up the string beans & kale.

Step 4 - Sauté the craisins, ginger, and onions together until you get them nice and golden brown.

Step 5 - Add the kale, string beans, and black eyed peas. Let it simmer.

Step 6 - Once the plantain is done, remove the skin and mash up. Add the sea salt and voila, it's like mashed potatoes!

Jamaican Traditional Dish
Serve with boiled spelt dumpling (spelt flour)

Serves 2-3 people
Prep time: 7 mins
Total time: 30 mins

Ingredients:
2 bunches Callaloo
1 Red Bell Pepper
1 Green Bell Pepper
1 Onions
1 Scotch Bonnet Pepper
½ tsp Ginger Powder
½ tsp Pink Himalayan Sea Salt

Instructions:
Step 1 - Cut up the callaloo, red pepper, onion and scotch bonnet pepper.
Step 2 - Sauté your ingredients.
Step 3 - After they simmer together, add the callaloo and cook for fifteen minutes.

Raw Quinoa Salad

Serves 4-6 people
Prep time: 10 mins
Total time: 22 mins

Ingredients:
1 Onions
1 Jalapeño
2 Tomatoes
1 can Black beans
1 can Chickpeas
1 bunch Spinach
1 bunch Kale
5 leaves Cilantro (or 1 tbspn dried)
1 Avocado
1 inch of Ginger
1 Red Onion
5 leaves Parsley (or 1 tbspn dried)
Spicy jalapeño avocado sauce (recipe in back)

Instructions:
Step 1 - Open your cans of beans and wash and soak them in cold water to help get rid of the preservatives. After soaking and washing put them on the side to dry.
Step 2 - Put your quinoa to cook. Once it's done put it on the side to cool.
Step 3 - Prepare your sauce: blend all your ingredients together get a nice creamy sauce. If you want it more creamy add more grapeseed oil.
Step 4 - Dice up all your herbs and tomatoes.
Step 5 - Put them together with the beans and quinoa. Mix it together and add your sauce.

Curry Chickpeas with Boiled Bananas

Serves 4 people
Prep time: 3 mins
Total time: 15 mins

Ingredients:
2 Green Bananas
½ lb bag Collard Greens
1 large can Chickpeas
2 tsp Curry
3 Scallion
1 inch Ginger

Instructions:
Step 1 - Cut the ends off your banana and slice in half.
Step 2 - Put them to boil.
Step 3 - When bananas turn dark, remove from water and peel.
Step 4 - Wash and cut up collard greens (add red onion to spice it up!).
Step 5 - Massage grapeseed oil into collard greens. Set aside.
Step 6 - Wash in cold water and pre-cook your chickpeas for five minutes to reduce preservatives.
Step 7 - Sauté the chickpea with curry seasoning, scallion, and ginger. Let it simmer.

Falafel Burger with the Yucca Fries

Serves 4 people
Prep time: 3 mins
Total time: 15 mins

Ingredients:
1 large can Chickpeas
5 leaves Parsley
1 Red Onion
½ tsp Cumin
1 inch Ginger
1 large Yucca

Instructions:
Step 1 - If you're using canned chickpeas, wash and soak them in cold water, then put on the side to dry.

Step 2 - Cut your yucca into wedges or french fry shapes. Cook them in grapeseed oil over medium heat. Take them out and drain them when they turn golden brown.

Step 3 - Dice up the parsley, onions and ginger.

Step 4 - Blend the dried chickpeas with your diced up herbs in a food processor.

Step 5 - Form a nice chickpea patty. If it's too moist, add spelt flour to firm.

Step 6 - You can bake them (350 degrees for 30-35 minutes) or fry them. I prefer to fry them because I like that crispy outer shell.

Sautéed Walnut Meat
Serve with red rice and a nice Spicy mango sauce

Serves 4 people
Prep time: 10 mins
Total time: 30 mins

Ingredients:
1 cup Walnuts
1 can Chickpeas
1 Onion
1 Scallions
1 inch Ginger

Instructions:
Step 1 - Soak walnuts for hour an half.
Step 2 - Wash and soak chickpeas in cold water.
Step 3 - Wash and boil the rice.
Step 4 - Drain the water from the walnuts. They should feel soft and gummy like meat.
Step 5 - Dice up the ginger, scallions, and onions.
Step 6 - Sauté the walnut meat with the chickpeas and herbs. Add more seasoning if desired.

Black Bean Lentil Burger
With Roasted Sweet Potato Bun

Serves 5-6 people
Prep time: 10 mins
Total time: 45 mins

Ingredients:
½ lb Lentils
1 can Black Beans
2 inches Ginger
1 Red Onion
Large Sweet Potato
Grapeseed Oil
Spicy Avocado Sauce (recipe in back)

Instructions:
Step 1 - Preheat your oven 300° then slice your large sweet potato.
Step 2 - Grease the pan with grapeseed oil and then add sweet potato. Let them bake for 20 mins, then flip and cook for another 15-20 minutes. Done when they are softened but still firm.
Step 3 - Cook your lentils until they are soft but not mushy. Once they are done, drain them and put them on the side.
Step 4 - Drain your can of black beans and rinse them in cold water. Put them on the side to dry.
Step 5 - Dice up the onions, ginger, and scallion.
Step 6 - Grab a bowl to mix your cooked lentils, dry black beans, and diced up ingredients, or add them all to a food processor.
Step 7 - Form your black bean patty with your hands. If it's too moist, add spelt flour to bind it together.
Step 8 - Bake on 350 degrees or fry in grapeseed oil over medium heat.

Good to top with dandelion grrens!

SNACKS AND MUNCHIES

Burro Banana Wedges

Serves 1-2 people
Prep time: 2 mins
Total time: 12 mins

Ingredients:
Burro Banana
½ tsp Cayenne Pepper
½ tsp Sea Salt
Grapeseed Oil

Instructions:
Step 1 - Cut the burro banana into wedges and put into a bowl.
Step 2 - Add your seasoning to give them a nice coating.
Step 3 - Grab your cast iron frying pan and lightly coat with grapeseed oil.
Step 4 - Fry banana until lightly browned on each side.

Fried Green Plantains

Serves 1-2 people
Prep time: 2 mins
Total time: 12 mins

Ingredients:
2 Green Plantains
2 tablespoons Grapeseed Oil
Optional: Sea Salt

Instructions:
Step 1 - Peel and cut diagonally or round, into 1/4-inch-thick slices.
Step 2 - Drizzle just enough oil into a nonstick skillet to coat the bottom of the pan and place it on medium heat.
Step 3 - When the oil begins to shimmer, but not smoke, add plantains (work in batches) and fry for 1 1/2 minutes on one side, flip and cook for 1 minute on the other side.
Step 4 - Remove plantains from pan and drain on paper towels.
Step 5 - Continue frying in batches until all the plantains are fried.

Ital smoothie

Serves 2 people
Prep time: 2 mins
Total time: 5 mins

Ingredients:
1 Cucumber
5 leaves Watercrest
½ tsp Turmeric
1 Banana
1 stalk Bok Choy
1 tsp of Sea Moss Gel
Kale
5 leaves Dandelion
3 Dates
½ tsp Maca root
½ tsp Kelp Powder
½ tsp Bladderwrack
3 leaves of Collard Greens

Instructions:
Step 1 - Dice up all your ingredients.
Step 2 - Add it to your blender, not a juicer.
Step 3 - Blend it together and enjoy that motherfucker!

Strawberrie Sorbet

Serves 3 people
Prep time: 2 mins
Total time: 5 mins

Ingredients:
Frozen Strawberries
Frozen Banana
½ tsp Coconut Flakes
½ tsp Chia Seeds

Instructions:
Step 1 - Blend strawberries and bananas in a food processor.
Step 2 - Put mixture into a bowl.
Step 3 - Add the chia seeds and coconut flakes on top.

SAUCES

Tamarind Chutney/Tamarind Sauce

Serves 20 people
Prep Time: 5 mins
Total Time: 25 mins

Ingredients:
1/2 Tamarind seeded
1/2 cup Date Sugar
2 cups Boiling Water
1-1/2 tbsp Roasted Ground Cumin Seeds
1 tsp Black Salt
1 tsp Red Chili Powder
1 tsp Ground Black Pepper
1/2 tsp Ginger Powder

Instructions:
Step 1 - Break the tamarind into small pieces and soak in boiling hot water for one hour.
Step 2 - Strain and mash into a pulp. Remove the seeds.
Step 3 - Add date sugar to the pulp. Mix well.
Step 4 - Add the remaining ingredients. Mix and taste.
Step 5 - Add more date sugar, salt, or pepper as needed.

Sweet Heat Date Sauce

Serves 6 people
Prep Time: 2 mins
Total Time: 2 mins

Ingredients:

6 Dates
½ tsp Crushed Chili Pepper
1 Lime
1 Ginger
2 tsp Grapeseed Oil

Instructions:

Step 1 - Soak dates for 30 mins in hot or warm water.
Step 2 - Blend all the ingredients together.

Spicy Avocado Sauce

Serves 4 people
Prep Time: 2 mins
Total Time: 2 mins

Ingredients:
1 Avocado
1 Scotch Bonnet Pepper
1 Ginger
1 Lime
2 tsp Grapeseed Oil

Instructions:

Step 1
Step 1 - Peel and chop up the ingredients.

Step 2 - Combine in a blender and blend on low until creamy.

Mango Chutney

Serves 4-5 people
Prep time: 5 mins
Total minutes: 7 mins

Ingredients:
2 Mangoes
1-2 Limes
2 Onions
1 Parsley
1 Ginger
1 Scotch Bonnet Pepper
2 tsp Grapeseed Oil

Instructions:
Step 1 - Dice up 1 mango and 1 onion and set aside.
Step 2 - Blend all other ingredients in a food processor or blender.
Step 3 - After well blended, add diced mango and onion.

Can stay refrigerated for 4-5 days.

Notes

Notes

Made in United States
North Haven, CT
22 March 2024

50351666R00042